STARTUP

Resources You Need to Master Product Launches

(An Accelerated Guide to Thinking Just Like a
Successful Startup)

Lucille Kaplan

Published By Jordan Levy

Lucille Kaplan

Startup: Resources You Need to Master Product Launches

(An Accelerated Guide to Thinking Just Like a Successful

Startup)

ISBN 978-1-77485-349-8

Legal & Disclaimer

The information contained in this book is not designed to replace or take the place of any form of medicine or professional medical advice. The information in this book has been provided for educational and entertainment purposes only.

The information contained in this book has been compiled from sources deemed reliable, and it is accurate to the best of the Author's knowledge; however, the Author cannot guarantee its accuracy and

tort, negligence, personal injury, criminal intent, or under any other cause of action.

You agree to accept all risks of using the information presented inside this book. You need to consult a professional medical practitioner in order to ensure you are both able and healthy enough to participate in this program.

TABLE OF CONTENTS

Introduction

Making the choice to strike off on your own and establish a brand new business requires both vision and courage in equal measures. It requires a lot of dedication, hard work and a complete grasp of the steps needed along with a bit of luck in order for the company to start off on the start.

The essentials necessary to help take your dream idea of starting a business from vision and into the next chapters. The first step is to learn ways to generate concepts. Then, this monograph will go into the nitty gritty of forming a legitimate business and also building an effective team.

In the next section, you'll be taught how to build websites and build an identity to give your company the online exposure it needs. The final part will discuss the most effective methods for marketing that show your clients that you're an authority in your chosen field.

There are a lot of books about this topic that are available, thank you for choosing this book! The best effort was put into make pages filled with helpful details. Enjoy!

Chapter 1: How to Handle Your

Employees

In this section you'll learn about the strategies that you can employ to work on behalf of your workers. As the manager of a business that is just starting out it is essential to be able to lead to train and motivate your employees. You must work with other people . Even the most skilled managers and entrepreneurs cannot work in isolation. Read this article carefully for a smooth and harmonious relationship. peace of mind with your team members.

An idea from a professional

Richard Branson, one of the most well-known entrepreneurs around the world considers that the employees of a company are essential to the company's success and longevity. Branson stated that businesses are, at their core, groups of people who share the same goal. Therefore, entrepreneurs must learn how to be an efficient leader.

According to his observations, employees are similar to flowers. They blossom when they are given the right amounts of praise and guidance. A leader must be able to inspire, listen, and praise his team members.

The Strategies You Can Apply

This section of the book will provide you with practical strategies. The strategies you'll discover here will allow you become a more effective leader for your staff.

Utilizing Positive Feedback

This is a rule of thumb is important to keep in mind that positive wording is the greatest motivational tool for employees. This means that you must include positive feedback to your entrepreneurial toolbox. Praise can motivate your employees to strive for excellence.

Some entrepreneurs fail to utilize this effective instrument. If you're not comfortable using positive language in our company, you can use the following strategies:

Make Your Employees Feel Appreciated as Quickly as You Can - Similar to every other business venture it is essential to take action immediately whenever you want to congratulate your employees. Offer positive feedback as quickly after you have noticed your employees' positive actions.

Make it Public The best way to do this is to praise your employees in front of their colleagues. Recognize your employee's achievement whenever you can.

Indicate What They Did Correctly Positive feedback without explaining why could be just as damaging as a lack of appreciation. When you are expressing your opinion on employees, you must identify the exact activities you're discussing.

Make it a habit to give praise frequently Don't need to wait until you have achieved a huge feat before you give positive feedback. If you wish to inspire your employees, make sure you make appropriate remarks about the small things they do.

Make sure your employees are engaged

Many employees do not enjoy their work. People are known to be ill physically, psychologically, as well as emotionally while working.

As the head for an enterprise, it is your responsibility to ensure that your employees are happy to the greatest extent you can. It's true that each person is accountable for their satisfaction and happiness. But, if you want your employees to be effective, productive as well as efficient, then you have to ensure that they are active in what they're doing.

Happier employees are usually more productive than colleagues who are unhappy. You've probably guessed that if someone is satisfied then he'll show less absence, more productive work, and provide better customer service. The most successful entrepreneurs adhere to this basic principle Employee engagement is directly linked to the happiness and satisfaction of employees.

However that, you should not "please" your employees in a blatant manner. Instead, you should adopt methods that are passive and can improve the overall satisfaction of your company startup. The next technique, dubbed "RESPECT," will help to keep your employees motivated and engaged.

The RESPECT Technique

The technique is comprised of seven components that are:

Recognition - You must be sure to acknowledge and reward the employees you employ for their efforts.

Empowerment - You must empower your employees to allow them to accomplish their work effectively. Management is a great way to enable your employees through providing them with training and the appropriate tools.

Support - Leaders need to be able to support their subordinates. You're the boss of your company, so you need to be a supportive and competent leader for your staff. Be sure to offer them ongoing education and mentorship.

Partnership Employees will be more engaged when they feel they play an important part in the business. So, it is important to consider the employees you employ as partners the running of your business , regardless of their position.

Expectations - Discuss your expectations with employees. This method assists you keep your staff up-to-date with the demands of the company. In addition, you must define goals your employees are expected to meet. They are accountable for their achievement of these goals.

Be considerate - Treat all staff member as a fellow human being. In certain instances, managers think of their employees as replacements for tools to accomplish certain tasks. In the end, this can affect employee motivation and the overall culture of the workplace.

Trust - Your employees have met the standards you set in your hiring procedure. They are therefore equipped to perform the tasks you want to ask them to do. The most successful entrepreneurs are able to trust their employees. It is best if you allow your employees to make decisions that are appropriate for their specific job.

Chapter 2: Establishing An Online

presence

In many cases experts and authority are usually used interchangeably. This isn't the case with online marketing, however, since being an authority is essential as being an authority is better than simply occupying second position. In this instance experts are those who has a deep understanding of specific areas of expertise, and an authority is the one who all the specialists agree on is the primary destination for information regarding specific niches. In other words authorities aren't considered to be authorities simply since they claim to be experts, they're authorities since when they announce their opinions regarding their field that they choose, others take note.

While being recognized as an expert in your field seems incredible, there are more tangible benefits of being aware that you will have a voice heard by the people you choose to target. In particular, if you're recognized as an authority in your field you will be able to count on many eyes to be on your shop and an army of faithful supporters who are inclined to follow your example. This means that in this situation, you'll be able not have to worry about finding ways to increase your reach and be assured that people in your chosen field will be looking for you instead.

The most important part in this is to build trust between you and your client base. A person who is a authority figure gains authority, not just by doing things right every now and then but by being consistent every time, regardless of what. If you do this consistently for long enough, and those who respect your example will begin to accept your word as truth immediately. If you get sufficient to the point where you've gained trust from the very beginning and respect it with the most reverence and never try to harm it regardless of what.

Prepare yourself

Do the research you need to do: There's no method to gain information about your area of expertise the only thing that is required is dedication to conducting the research that is needed. Researching means getting information from trustworthy sources that includes the academic literature, and not only going through the pertinent Wikipedia pages, although they are a great starting point in the event that the sites that you visit contain credible sources. If you're conducting your research you will discover that there isn't a single piece of information that is too small and there is no trivia you do not need to learn. The more data you can gather together the more useful. Do not be afraid to take notes and use them often when you're creating material that you are proud of.

Begin with a limit in the pursuit of becoming an authority on an area that you know about, it's essential to set achievable goals for yourself to be sure that you're working towards a realistic objective. Instead of striving to become an authority on all things related to your field and then focusing on learning every aspect of a specific vertical portion of it. The more targeted your study is focused, the more flexibility you'll have, and the simpler for you to gain an understanding of the subject you're tackling. Keep in mind that a jack-of all trades is a master at none.

Be aware of your competitors There are some major players in your area that you researched prior to making a commitment to a particular target, it's crucial to be aware of who your competitor is in the space of authority around your field. It should not be difficult. All you have be doing is look for your area on Google and search for the names that pop up the frequently. After this has been done you'll have to determine if you'd prefer to challenge them or take to a particular segment of the field instead. Whatever the level of ensconcement the other person is, there's always room for an additional expert in the field and you might require going further than you have to in finding out where the room actually lies.

Make a guideline: Although it might appear to be a strange suggestion for you to create guides while still in the process of learning, you will be amazed by the efficacy as a tool for learning it could be. This will not only produce important material that can be used in many different ways in the future and also ensure that you're extremely familiar with the content all over, which can aid in retention quite quickly. Additionally, you'll be able to master the concepts behind them more thoroughly when you are required to use on the information that is relevant in its most fundamental format.

Additionally, the format you develop for your guide can be later used to create additional outline templates to be used in future material, making it simpler to develop an outline of every piece of content you'll create to achieve the goal of being recognized as an authority. When you are laying out these particulars it is vital that you are able to present the information in a manner that even someone who is completely uninitiated about the subject will be able to comprehend what you're saying. No matter how knowledgeable about a subject you're knowledgeable If you're unable to express your thoughts clearly, then your credibility in the field isn't going to rise.

Join in with your target audience

The ability to know everything you can about a certain subject is one thing, but being viewed as an authority is a different. To be seen as an authority, you must be perceived by people who are in the community as a definitively the one. This implies that in addition to being capable of walking the talk as well, you're able to communicate your message. It is essential to utilize the right language and to strike the right cultural touchstones, and also be a part of the population you're trying to reach. Even if you don't meet the criteria it is essential to establish an identity that fits without a shadow of doubt.

The most effective way to accomplish this is to dig into the demographic information you discovered when you created your plan for business. If your target demographics are younger than 30, Then you should head to YouTube to see what influential influencers in your niche have to say about their lives, literally. Take note of how they speak, what subjects they cover and what their opinions are about the current state of affairs. day.

If your market is targeted towards an older audience, the information you have learned in your studies should be sufficient to provide you with an idea of what the market expects. If you are in an older audience it is recommended to look for similar phrases on YouTube and then watch the content produced by the creators of content with the most views. Knowing what they sound like will make your content appear more authentic and therefore more credible since your viewers will feel that it's an authentically created content by the same source as a friend.

Once you've got a sense of who your target audience should be, you should think about the impressions of your people and then consider the goal of your blog's content. The goal should be particular, not just increasing traffic to your site which means you can generate more customers for your company, and these goals could change as time passes. For instance, at first your aim could be to build a large following on social media, however later you might decide to advertise certain new products when they come out.

After you have identified the goals you want to achieve, you'll be able later to identify which tone to convey your message.

Informal: It's best to avoid informal language from the beginning since new readers could be turned off by what may feel like an inauthentic familiarity. It's okay to incorporate the style over time, but you'll need to ensure that you maintain your authority while doing so. The best method to achieve this is to remain engaged and passionate about the subject matter, and mixing more in-depth information and more casual phrasing.

Promotional: Although you will definitely want to advertise new products or services when they are released It is possible to return to this frequently when you're not careful, that's why it's crucial to be cautious when publishing this kind of content at the beginning of your site since you don't want visitors who visit your website to believe that it's just a collection of long ads for your goods. Whatever content you create it is crucial to remain your authority by providing specific, specific motives that make the product or services you're selling worthwhile to your customers.

Formal formal: This is the style you're likely to use when you begin creating content for your blog. Although it's certainly acceptable in the beginning however, you should transition into something slightly more casual in time, as you wish your readers to feel like they are speaking with a friend every time engaging with the posts and not feel like they are listening to a lecture. While this may be a good method to sound like you're an authoritative figure it's the kind of authority figure who people pay attention to because they have been pressured to listen to and not because they wish to. An alternative over time is to make your content enjoyable and interesting for your readers as you can while also providing relevant, informative content that can make people see you as an authority that they can trust.

Create your own blog

If you want to become an authority within your area, you must to create content you want to share with others. This requires having an unwavering voice, with content that gives something that people in the niche you choose can't discover elsewhere. When you write, it's crucial to remember that while there's a lot of experts in your area who are able to explain the information in question, the thing that keeps people returning repeatedly is your writing.

If you're unable to choose a tone of voice the best place to start is the personality the brand has. Look over the best descriptions you have come up with and then set aside time pondering the how you can convey these traits on a regular basis through what you write. The options for bringing a personal sound and feel to your writing are things like sprinkling your writing with original references, switching subjects frequently or tangents.

Examine the way you talk naturally and think about ways to let it be evident through your written work. Consider the way you write your sentences, sentences length and punctuation use. In the end, do not create your personal style emerge immediately, as it is likely to develop organically over time.

Make a plan: Once you are ready to begin creating content on a regular basis, you're agreeing to a substantial increase in the workload since the content requires updates several times per week. This involves taking a seat and creating between 30-50 content ideas that are of different lengths and require various amounts of work before writing. A typical blog post should be between 500 and 700 words however, you should try to run every week a longer piece and at least two times the length.

This is the reason it's crucial to keep an agenda of articles you'll be writing, along with another piece of content you must create in one go to be prepared for the instances when the other content doesn't come together in a timely manner or when you think you require to take a break. Once you have started your blog it is essential to make sure it doesn't fall to stale as nothing could make the appearance of a site as if it's been abandoned better as much as a blog that hasn't been updated for one year or more.

Spread the word in the early days of your blog may be a little crowded with readers. However, that doesn't mean your post will never be read. Each post you write should be made available to the social media world and should include a request for readers to share the articles they enjoy in addition. Remember that all your social media profiles are easily visible at the bottom of your screen at all times.

It is, above all, important to remember that it is crucial to keep your eyes open throughout this time as currently it is far more important to create a lot of content that showcases your skills than for the content to instantly begin generating sales. Keep in mind that being an expert is a strategy for marketing that will pay off over the long run In other words you can think as a marathon not a sprint. Slow and steady will win the race.

Make sure you get the word out

After you've created some months of material, it'll finally be time to display the world how much you've learned. To get started you should find the most popular forums that are populated by people who have concerns about your field and become an active participant. Answer questions, respond to relevant posts and make your own blog, and each when you do, you should credit the information to your blog. At this point, it's crucial to not promote or promote your own products or services. At this stage Being an authority isn't all about direct marketing and the sales that follow occur naturally and forcing it will only delay the process.

When you begin to see some the results of this promotion Begin to reach out to other experts within the community who have their own websites to offer your services as part of an article for guest bloggers. It is well-known that the production fresh content may be a major stress and typically it is the case that the other party will gladly accept your offer so long as you prove that you're a pro. On the surface creating top-quality content for competitors is a risky option. Under the surface, however it's extremely beneficial because of a number of reasons.

There's nothing more likely to strengthen the impression that customers think that you're an authority in your field than having another person to give their approval by allowing you to publish material on their site. The only thing you have to do is write appealing, high-quality contentand include an url to your website at the conclusion of the article. If you do it right then you'll be able to entice your competition's customers by gaining their consent. In order to seal the deal, you launch a hefty campaign after the new content is up to give new eyes to your site an incentive to take a look at your site more closely.

Chapter 3: Data-Driven Approach

Data Driven Approach eliminates bottlenecks in the workflow process by collecting all data that impacts the flow. The data is fed to the computer system and utilize sophisticated Lean Analytics to understand the nature of the issue and identify possible solutions. Data analysis helps to discover hidden details that manual inspections could miss. This is the principal reason for using data-driven analytics.

The other aspect of the The second aspect of the Data-Driven Approach is the amount of change and the amount that the system needs to undergo to ensure optimal performance. Modifying an element's value in one method could boost the profits of the company. But, it could also be detrimental to other factors that affect the flow. We employ data analytics to analyze the effects of changes and to determine how we can manage each aspect in accordance with the needs of the company.

Improved performance in the workplace should result from the development that each individual. This is the premise of the Lean method. It alters thinking so that the notions of gain and money disappear in the wake of quality and the addition of values. What is the best way to define the line? This is the most important problem that the lean professional is faced with when trying to apply the data-driven strategy in the workplace.

The framework for the data-driven Lean Transformation

There are a variety of ready-made models that you can use to create your own framework. They've evolved by constant use and evolution and therefore have a high degree of stability and reliability that is built-in. You can create the framework of your choice by taking on the problems you wish to resolve using the framework.

What's the issue that impacts us in a significant way?

What is the fundamental structure of our society today? Are we able to drive it or alter it?

What type of change that we will bring to our work?

Does the new system of working call for changes to the management system? Are we in need of changes to the way that leaders behave?

What is the best method we can use to enhance our capability?

These questions pertain to the framework on the macro and micro levels. The responsibility of each person is different with each level based on the size of the framework. The system should take care of all related issues which include those dealing with interrelations between the various aspects. If it fails to do so it, the change could be slowed down.

The solution to the problems

To begin, you must address the problem you're facing. It could be about establishing yourself within the local market and finding a suitable location to establish your business or deciding on a suitable name. Develop a hypothetical solution and use Lean techniques to get rid of the ones that aren't efficient. Most often this is the start point for a company which is why you have to tackle this issue and resolve it fully.

If you're not happy with the location you are in or don't have a space to run your business, you should look around for a different location. You could lease out your current space or use the space of an existing company. If you are looking for suggestions to name your business then you should look on the web. There are numerous websites which offer ideas for names.

Structure of the current culture

It is based on the location you live. If you're a resident of the area, then there will be no difficulties integrating. The process of transportation as well as distribution is based on the local customs and practices of the region. If you're not acquainted with these practices, you won't have many customers in this area.

The process of implementing is easy. The user is able to gather the data to be used with the website. The use pattern will vary for every user. It is possible to add additional elements to your site to increase the usability and conversion. Thus, a framework is built. Feedback from users will provide an insight into the performance of the site and what changes you'd like to make.

We examine the work-related details for a specific type of user. Lean programming allows us to select the appropriate parameters for the usage for the program. The performance is evaluated and, if it receives positive results it is then it is then the amount of people multiplied. If the performance is acceptable, other users are added to the test. The test continues until there is an overall positive reaction to the test by the person.

The Data You Need for Your Analytics

Analytics is a measurement of how far one has come towards their goals. It is important to know your goals before you consider the use of a measurement. This has been done before however, here are some other things to know.

The most fundamental step to create a successful measurement is to collect adequate quantities of accurate data. The data has to meet certain standards and characteristics. The qualifications and requirements are:

Comparable

A single piece of data provides little details. For instance, the sale of three items today isn't providing much or any useful data. It's impossible to gauge the progress you've made on your own.

It provides you with a starting point. However, it requires an additional source of information to make it useful in tracking your growth.

Let's say you've sold three products today, and you sold nine yesterday. You can get more precise data from that circumstance.

It is possible to synthesize two data points, and then evaluate the result. It is possible to find out that your product was not performing as well in comparison to yesterday. Take note of comparable data points to evaluate your performance.

Understandable

If you're not able to grasp the significance of a particular data point the data point becomes meaningless. For instance, if you reside in the UK you'll be more familiar with miles than miles.

Ask an American what distance a location is from the point you're at. Expect him to give you a distance figure by using Imperial miles.

The answer you'll get is right and is true. But, it's not as important since you may not have an clue how long the mile actually is.

As a result it is important to be able process data in a way that makes it understandable as well as pertinent. This quote is frequently used to refer to Einstein, "It should be possible to explain the principles of physics to an employee at a bar."

In fact, Ernest Rutherford said that. If that's the case then you'll be able to comprehend and explain the information you have gathered.

Rate-able

A data point can be converted and translatable into numbers. It must always take shape of percentage or ratio. In the end, you should transform the raw information or data into a the form of a ratio or percentage.

For instance, you sold three phones yesterday , and nine today. It's much easier and more informative when you analyze the information using percentages or ratios. There ia an increase of 300% in sales of phones in your retail store right now.

However, it is important to be cautious when it comes to this. The author William Bruce Cameron said it best in his book Informal Sociology: A Brief Introduction into Sociological Thinking "Not every thing that could be counted counts. And not all that counts can be counted."

Relevant

As previously mentioned the metric or data has to be of a high-quality. A relevant metric could make your mind think about improvements or modifications. A non-relevant metric is worth knowing.

The customer purchased three items from your business today. You can certainly understand what it signifies. But does it mean anything? Does it have any significance? What was the purchase made by the client? It's actually easy to understand. The information is straightforward the customers purchased three items from you.

It is irrelevant since it lacks any information or context. It's not accompanied by any data to be considered relevant as an metric. If you're collecting data that is understandable it is best to ensure that your data points be specific and precise.

For instance, a customer purchased three iPhone units from your retail store. The context shifts and you can see the importance of the data. You can see whether your iPhone models are getting more well-known than other phones you have in your store.

Keep in mind that it's wiser to accumulate more data , and get rid of the extra. With less data, it limits you to the things you can discover.

Eight types of data

This is where it becomes fascinating. It is important to understand that you have at a minimum eight kinds of data. It is possible to use them to create a business measure to gauge your company's growth. The majority of lean analytics utilize the first two types to create the sole metric that's important.

It will help out if you are aware of the eight types of data to keep you from making a mistake when using the data types in a way that isn't appropriate. Other types, in addition to quantitative and qualitative, can aid in the creation of unique metrics. These metrics may not aid in measuring the progress of your business, but they can assist you with other tasks like marketing, company management, and so on.

Qualitative

These include customer interviews, or anything else that doesn't require numbers. It can take the form of gut feelings or even personal feedback. This provides you with insight. This lets you consider ways to gather or gather information for the next kind of measurement.

Qualitative data is typically transformed into quantitative. For example, feedback data can be transformed into numbers, for example: 5 for positive feedback, and 0 , for negative. The effectiveness of a product is assessed in this manner.

But data in its qualitative form can be beneficial when it comes to lean analytics. Comments from customers can aid in the development process of your products.

Quantitative

It's mostly data. This is the most commonly used kind of data that companies use regardless of whether they're running slim or not. The information you gather from this kind of metric will allow you to understand the information you require to collect.

Unlike qualitative, you can't easily revert quantitative data to qualitative. The only thing one can accomplish is interpret it.

Data can be modified or distorted by interpretation.

Astonishment

It's just a way to feel great. It doesn't help you develop strategies that will benefit your business. In fact, it's frequently employed as a measure to gauge the progress of your business. It's still an effective motivator and marketing tool for companies.

Affordable

It is often gathered from within your company. But it can also be gathered through customer feedback also. Data and metrics that can be used to make decisions will provide you with insight. These insights directly impact and affect your business's decision-making.

Exploratory

This is speculational data that's created with the current data available that is available. This could involve predictions of the way metrics alter in the future. It also shows how metrics can be altered to get the desired result.

Reports

The information gathered from reports could be useful as well as exploratory, vanity or even lagging. It is generated by employees or source it from third-party sources. It is usually bought by companies on a regular basis dependent on the way you decide to set it up.

Lagging

The majority of people refer to lagging data in the form of historical information. It is not possible for all data to be acquired immediately. Certain business decisions need time to observe the results. The results are interpreted as useful data.

Leading

The most significant distinction between leading and exploratory data is the period of time it anticipates. Exploratory data tend to be predictions that are based on the distant future. Leading is expected for data in the near future.

Chapter 4: Graphic Designer

Do you have a flair for aesthetics? Are you driven enough to make an extra income through your talents?

Evaluate your skills

What are you able to accomplish in the field of graphic design? A lot of graphic designers are expected to create:

Logos

Business cards for business

Website design

Social media design

Animation design

Stationary

Print design

Typography design

Packaging

Print

Restaurant

Infographics

Look up the competitors.

Study the graphic design competition within your region, particularly those competing with your clients.

Establish a price list

Are you planning for an hourly fee or be paid on a project-by- basis? Remember that you'll have permanent clients and temporary customers.

Be legal

Make a contract you can have your prospective clients fill out , which includes the following details:

Service requested

Delivery schedule

Estimated cost

Agreement between both parties

What is required by the customer

Transfer of rights to the completed materials

Limitation of liability

Cancellation policy

Outsource skills

With the advent of the internet, it's more convenient than ever to outsource a portion of larger projects in order to increase your capabilities and ensure that your clients are happy.

Make yourself known

As graphic designer, you must clearly create a personal brand in order to draw clients who be interested in working with you. People will instantly evaluate your skills based on what they perceive from your personal brand yourself.

Network

Graphic designers, like other similar professions, you will need to spend the most time you can to expand your relationships with your competition and potential clients. You need to be able easily share your business issues and gain from the knowledge of others in the same industry.

Online Dating Consultant

The advancements in technology have created an ever-growing demand for consultants working in the world of online dating. Online dating consultants assist people in navigating the world of online dating.

Contrary to what is commonly believed Many of these sites do not only serve to search for a spouse. Your task as consultant in this area is to fulfill a range of requirements, from either casual or serious. You're expected to form connections and strengthen relationships. You contribute to building a stronger community!

The day-to-day life of an online dating expert:

Meetings with clients

Editing and writing dating profiles

Making responses to messages

Taking profile photos

Advertising

Social media strategies

How to make money

In this type of work-from-home business, you'll usually charge clients for the time you spend. You must create a price that covers various levels of service for specified periods of time.

If you're gifted in identifying people and getting people to get connected with one another, your chances of business growth is substantial.

Skills required:

Know what people are looking for.

Don't be a judge of others.

Personable and friendly

Flexible enough to plan ahead

Organized

Ability to multitask

Costs to start

Beginning an online dating consultant business is not expensive to begin. It is unlikely that you will require many office supplies other than your computer! I recommend you make an online presence that promotes and highlights the services you offer and that's where your expenditure will occur. Budget $150 on a website advertising, as well as other advertising.

The steps to start your consulting business:

Make a business plan

Establish a legal business entity

Register for taxes

Set up a bank account devoted to business expenses

Establish an accounting system.

Get the license you need

Find business insurance

Your brand's identity should be defined to stand out

Establish a strong web presence

Affiliate Marketer

A highly effective and simplest ways to earn money online is to create an affiliate marketing company or incorporating affiliate marketing into the existing model of your business.

Is affiliate marketing a form of marketing?

Affiliate marketing lets you earn money online without having any website or personal product, by promoting and advertising products and services of others and receiving a percentage in the form of a commission in.

How to Launch an Affiliate Marketing Business

Select an affiliate network

It is essential to find the perfect match between your business and the one that will gain from your advertising initiatives. There are a myriad of affiliate networks available including the most well-known are Amazon, Apple, Google and Clickbank.

There are also entrepreneurs who have come up with amazing products worth a check out. A lot of companies have affiliate programs that you can sign up to for the purpose of promoting their products or services.

Find affiliate products and research them.

If you are a novice affiliate marketer, you require an effective strategy for your product. It is important to select an area that offers a variety of brands to select from. You should limit yourself or three products at a time in order to improve and become an expert that other people can consider reliable on the internet.

More comfortable get as an affiliate marketerthe easier easily you can delve into specific and broad areas.

Make sure you purchase the product before you promote it.

You're not required to buy items from companies before you promote them, but when you own and used something, it can help you establish credibility and confidence in the field that you're in. Furthermore, you'll know the exact specifications of the product, which could mean an enormous difference between making sales and not gaining potential customers.

I've found that writing reviews of products is an effective way to boost your reputation as an affiliate marketer regardless of the field you're in. Create case studies and share your own personal experiences with the products.

Make use of social media for more attention

There are a myriad of online traffic sources that are free to bring more visitors to your affiliate links

YouTube

Pinterest

Instagram

Twitter

Facebook

Snapchat

and many more! Video marketing is among the most well-known and effective because it is capable of demonstrating products rather than just reading the comments and looking at images.

Social Media Manager

Social media was an enjoyable method of connecting with people you cherish. Nowadays, it has transformed into a cost-effective method to advertise businesses in all sizes and shapes. There are many businesses that are overwhelmed by the work involved in managing various social media platforms and this is the perfect opportunity to benefit as an business owner!

What is a social media manger?

If you are a social media coordinator You provide services your clients require including but not only:

Staying up-to-date with the latest fashions

Posting images and other content

Set up of accounts

Making market strategies based upon your client's objectives

Growing the number of followers

Customer service

Marketing analysis

Community facilitation

What are the steps to become a social media administrator?

Knows the importance of the social media landscape as well as how they can be utilized as a tool for marketing

Has a deep understanding of the nuances on different platforms

Is able to devise strategies to achieve the goals and expectations of the client.

Captures the client's voice using illustrations and well-written content

Manages several platforms of media for a variety of customers

How to start an online business for a social media manager:

Make yourself known on social media

In order to get clients who require your assistance, you must be working to build your own social media authority across a range of platforms. This requires more than having a huge number of followers. You need to create an audience that connects with your.

Examine social media

The technology of platforms is constantly changing so marketing changes too, and you have to be aware of developments and changes.

Choose the type of service you would like to provide

You may choose to offer a range of deals, or a full-service plan that includes everything from setting up the account(s) as well as making and posting content, as well as moderated comments on the forum.

Create your business plan

The strategy doesn't have to be overly complicated Just make sure you have an effective plan to assist you in building on the initial achievement.

Goals

Services

Assets and liabilities

Marketing

Competition

Choose the price

Social media professionals earn between $48,000 and $75,000 per year. If you're beginning a new company, it may take some time to realize the amount. Recommendations and testimonials can help to make more money.

Obtain licensing

You can obtain the proper permits or licenses by contacting your county or city about licensing for businesses.

Keep working on your strategy

After everything is set You must maintain momentum to keep getting and keeping customers. Networking is crucial in the business world and will be the best way to get your first clients.

Chapter 5: Step-by-Step Guide to

Setting Your Crowdfunding

Campaign

In this section, you'll discover the basic steps to crowdfunding online and how to begin your own campaign by making application of the basic steps.

Three Essential Stages

There are three major phases of every crowdfunding campaign. There is the pre-planning stage. The owner of the business gets together with his advisors, partners attorneys accountants, lawyers and other necessary people to present an investment concept. They create a marketing plan, as well as the memorandum of offer. After they've formulated that they can then publish their offering on an online crowdfunding platform.

The next step is when they solicit funds. Investors post updates on funding and social media posts status updates, and they also respond to investor inquiries on the internet. Brokers contact potential investors and media. All parties must conduct due diligence throughout the process.

The public, on the other hand, will look the deal and then make investments. When the investments are made the money is transferred to an escrow account at a bank that can be FDIC insured. Notifications are sent out to media, investors and other parties concerned. If the goal capital is reached or exceeded, which can happen a lot of times, the crowdfunding portal informs escrow about the successful closing and enters the third phase.

The portal then distributes fees and commission blotters out to broker. The escrow sends the money to the founding company. The company maintains its relationship with investors, by offering the investors with their returns according to the schedule. The business then continues to function, which means recruiting employees, locating business partners, making customers and earning profits.

In a nutshell Here are the most important actions you must follow when launching and managing the crowdfunding campaign:

Step 1: Establish the foundation for your Project

The work must begin months prior to the launch of your campaign. The first step is to create the concept. After that, you need to develop a prototype of your product. You must ensure that the product is functioning before you begin the fundraising campaign. If you seek to raise money to fund ideas that are difficult to implement, your supporters will be extremely disappointed and could be able to accuse the organization of operating a scam.

Additionally, you must create an online presence, an approximate budget, and an effective marketing strategy. Make sure you prepare your taxes as well as other legal documents. These are the essentials for beginning with a sound company, and running crowdfunding projects are not any different. The importance of diligence is.

Step 2: Get Started on your Social Media Campaign / Other forms of marketing

There are people who frequently browse crowdfunding sites to find exciting new projects. But, you'll get more attention and also increase the number of investors, by making use of the social networks to benefit you. Consider this to be similar to marketing your products, business or services. It involves the same tactics and goals Spread the word about your campaign and make it easier for people to join by investing.

Step 3: Pick the most popular Crowdfunding website.

There are a number of differentcrowdfunding platforms today. Therefore, you must select the one that is working best for you. If you're looking to raise funds to support social causes You should consider RocketHub, Crowdrise, and Causes. If you're running an enterprise that involves creative ideas It is recommended to use Pubslush, Indiegogo, and Kickstarter. If you're looking for large ticket investors to fund your business then you should consider crowdfunding platforms like Fundable, AngelList, and Somolend.

Step 4: Determine A Goal for Funding

This is perhaps the most challenging aspect to your crowdfunding campaign. Certain crowdfunding platforms such as Kickstarter will not permit users to retain the funds even if you've not attained your goal of funding. It is therefore crucial to set realistic fundraising goals. Some projects have been able to raise more than a million dollars of investments. However, the majority of projects, particularly those with a new name within the field, achieve at least ten thousand dollars. Sometimes, it's less.

Step 6: Set Reward Tiers

What's the benefit for investors? Naturally, there should be some perks for those who invest into your company. In most cases it is a tangible part of the plan, like first access to any prototypes you release. You could also give them a tiny share in the businessthe decision is contingent on the amount of money they offer as well as what you are able to provide as a startup business owner. Be careful not to promise anything you can't afford to offer.

Step 7: Create Your Pitch

To do this, you'll need to explain to people the details of your venture, the business you run and the person you are. It is essential to clearly explain why you need the money and what you want to accomplish with the plan you've set up. Text is fine however, adding images on your site is much better. Visuals can help you get the attention of readers, and give visitors to peek inside the project you're working on. Try to convey your enthusiasm for your project, and inform them about the rewards they'll receive for their efforts in the process.

8. Post Your Campaign Online

Be sure to use only one site to run your campaign. It will be easier to look for and users will not think you're trying to raise money from two different sources. Pick a platform you trust and that supports the type of project that you're working on and concentrate all your efforts on making sure that the word gets out about the project. Make sure your campaigns generate interest and work hard required to convince people to believe in your cause. It's not going to be simple, but it's achievable!

Tip 9: Always post Updates on your Facebook Page.

Not only does doing this increase your credibility, but it can also increase the amount of attention towards your venture. If investors sense that you're succeeding and working hard towards realizing your goals and what you intend to accomplish, it could encourage them to join in too. This is crucial to your current investors too. Of course, they will like to know how you are doing and whether they took the right decision in aiding you. Videos and photos are excellent for this.

Step 10: Conduct Research and Enhance Your Project

While you've got your crowdfunding campaign in place, people are bound to offer suggestions and comments about how you can enhance the product. Review all the feedback you get and ensure that you take into consideration all of them, both the good and negative. What's more, they are likely to be your future customers and balancing between your concept and the needs of the market will increase the value of your product. Customers will like having their voice heard in a company they've invested money in, so make sure that you respond to their emails in addition. Communication is helpful.

Chapter 6: Utilizing Lists

Another way to generate ideas is to make lists that are widely available online. This is an excellent option especially if you are in the motivation to begin your own business, but you want to study different industries in depth before you come up with ideas and decide.

The most effective method of studying industries is to first choose the services you can offer customers, consumers or customers. There are four types of what you could do such as Growing, Selling, Producing and servicing.

Manufacturing: Everything that requires the mass production of goods falls to this category. Also crafts that aren't mass produced but are made using raw materials are also included to this category, like carpentry, jewelry making or glass-making.

Selling: Selling is any type of trade can be conducted, for example, purchasing large quantities of product at a bargain and then selling it at a higher price by raising the price to make the profit margin. For instance, a automobile dealership, a business that deals in global trade (buy from overseas, then sell the item to the USA) or auctions is a good fit here.

Growing: Any activity that requires the care and waiting for animals before selling the animal off. For instance, a gardening business that grows flowers in a flower garden and selling them by the individual could fall under this category.

Servicing: Any field that requires the use of time and specific expertise of its management as well as its employees in exchange in exchange for money falls under this category. For instance, plumbing, consulting and legal are just a few examples of what you can avail.

These categories are essential since they provide you with the clearest picture of your objectives and also where your particular company is located, which makes the choice and creation of ideas more straightforward. Therefore, it is beneficial to keep these categories in your head.

Let's now go through step-by-step on how to make use of lists to come up with ideas.

Step 1: First , you have to look up lists of industries or business ideas.

http://www.entrepreneur.com/businessideas/index.html

http://www.smallbusinessnotes.com/starting-a-business/alphabetical-list-of-business-possibilities.html

You can also consider determining the size of the sector you're planning to enter is. The following website to learn more about the various the different sectors:

https://www.census.gov/econ/

On the left side you will see the sectors under the section 'Data by Sector'. Select the sector that you would like to investigate and then create reports for the particular section you have selected. This will let you know how big the industry that you're generating an idea for actually.

Step 2: If you've already chosen your business area of expertise (namely selling, producing Growing or Servicing) choose at least ten concepts from the list you're using. Write them on paper or record your ideas using Word.

If you aren't sure of the category you're looking for create the table with each category's columns as well as ideas inside the boxes. Choose up to 10 ideas to each one.

Step 3: Establish elimination criteria and classify from the most important to the least essential. There should be at least two criteria that won't prevent the concept from coming to reality. We don't want to eliminate the possibility of fantastic events happening simply because we lack faith. Take your time here as you will be left with suggestions that you truly want to implement and that are more or less achievable before you go to the next stage.

4. For every idea, consider the advantages and drawbacks. Is it too costly to develop the idea? Do you have the ability to realize the concept using your current knowledge or know-how?

You can also add positive aspects to an idea such as competitive advantages or the size of your target market (if your product is unique in any way and could increase market share over rivals).

Step 5: Review your list according to your criteria for elimination and then sort the list from lowest to most expensive. Remove any idea that is over the budget.

Use the second criteria to remove the ones that are not in the criteria.

Continue to use more criteria until arrive at an ultimate decision. If you're left with several options choices, choose the one that has the best-performing and positive criteria.

Step 6: Refine your concept and get it feasible for implementation. Create an outline of your business plan if plan to apply for financial support. When you are ready, consider the best way to produce the product or offer your services to ensure quality and affordable costs.

Chapter 7: Create Your Brand!

If you intend to be or are an entrepreneur, this is one term you must not forget. The work you do on your branding is the only thing that can differentiate you from your competition. Being an entrepreneur, you must work on your branding is just as crucial as working on the product itself. You might have a fantastic product, but failing to effort to improve your branding will not help your product in the market. The best concern is "what are the benefits of branding? And why should I care about it?"

What is a brand?

According to the American Marketing Association defines it in this way:

"A Brand is an identifier, phrase symbol, design, or any other element that distinguishes a seller's product or service from others."

In terms of the logos, names and ads are the items which create your brand. They also distinguish your products or services from those of others.

A brand may be defined as the image or perception that a person has every when they are thinking of business's name, products or services e.g. Coca-cola Pepsi, Guinness, and Apple.

BRANDING

What is a brand's job?

It tells your story well It tells your story. I wrote "sell the story of your life" rather than "tell the story of your life" since everyone can tell a story , but nobody can tell their story. Your brand shouldn't just be visible to people and feel, but it must also be something people can connect to. The chemistry should be felt immediately upon seeing it. It should feel like of a new conversation between two individuals that is so successful that it is as if they've known each other for quite a while. This way, you will be able to easily draw your customers.

It is a way to invite people to visit your business. Your brand's image should be inviting appealing, appealing and simple to keep. There is a certain amount of psychology at play. Be aware when selecting your colors e.g. bright colors look more appealing than darker hues. Your brand must entice customers to make them want to experience it, so you should send an invitation.

It will take you on a trip/to fulfill the promise: Your business is expected to expand with your customers. It faces the daunting task of not just making promises but also delivering promises. Your brand has to meet the demands of customers increase. It is important to remember that you don't just have to win loyalty maintain the customers' loyalty also. In this scenario, will maintain your name in the memory of the hearts of your customers.

Make a brand that guarantees that customers buy your product Your brand's main goal to not only draw consumers in, but also to convince consumers to purchase your product. Branding also has the aim of earning money for the business who created it. Develop your brand so that consumers eventually use the product or avail your service.

Make a brand that solves the problem: Nobody would want to be associated with a brand doesn't exist, which is the reason why your brand has to be solving a need. You need to focus to create a brand that solves problems; a item or service.

Why should I create a BRAND?

We've already discussed why branding is crucial However, it is important to be aware of the following aspects:

In order to differentiate your product and services from your competition, you must to establish your own brand.

To comprehend your business goals When you are developing your business plan strategic You must create an identity.

How can I BRAND MESELF?

Develop a brand identity for the brand: I refer to things such as a logo web site, colors, and colors, as I mentioned earlier.

Pricing: It's funny how the cost of your item can be a way to create the impression of a brand e.g. Parle-G biscuits are only sold for FCFA 25, and FCFA 50, in Cameroon. That's branding.

Partnerships and sponsorships: Certain businesses are known for sponsoring and partnering on various reality TV shows, football games and more e.g. DSTV. Another form of branding.

The experience in the store: How often customers are accustomed to seeing your brand displayed in retail stores can make a fantastic brand.

Design of packaging and product The reason for this could be in common with differences in shape, size, and the color of your product.

Communication and advertising: Certain firms have certain slogans and songs that they employ in every advertisement or other communication channel e.g. MTN - "everywhere you go."

You've got it, my friends. everything you must be aware of about branding. If you are starting your company on the right track ensure that you are branding your business.

Chapter 8: What to Find Jobs for

Start-Ups

"Your job will take up a significant portion of your day and the only way to be content is to do the things you think are excellent work. The only way to be successful at your work is to enjoy the work you do."

Steve Jobs, co-founder of Apple and Pixar

After you have learned all about the different abilities you require in order to be able to find a job as a start-up You are confident in your abilities to apply these abilities. When you go to search for jobs in the start-up sector, do you will only find some vague listings, if they exist? The search for a start-up position is as simple as locating the right corporate job. It is essential to know where to look , and there are a lot of start-ups coming up every day, it's more about knowing who you can contact.

Where can I find new jobs?

The process of gaining entry into the start-up business isn't easy. The community within the start-up sector is close-knit, it is essential to learn how to be accepted in the local community. This can be done in the same manner when looking to get the job of a major company. In a large business, you could depend on referrals or connections to gain access to the entrance, but it's your own experience that earns you the job and future promotions within the company. Even if you don't have all of the required experience large companies usually offer development and training courses which can keep you focused and getting on the right track.

Start-ups aren't afforded the luxury of offering education. If you don't have the knowledge or experience they're looking for then they'll move to someone else who already has it. Although this may seem harsh, the reality is that training requires time, and that's something that most startups do not have. This is particularly true because most are learning as proceed, particularly because the things that worked in the initial phases of their start-up may not be able to continue working when they advance.

Do you find a way to integrate into a group such as this when you've had no experience in the start-up world, have no contacts to make and don't even know where to start? While it isn't easy but there are plenty of methods to enter the start-up world even if you're just starting out.

First thing to do is start researching some of the most reputable start-ups from trustworthy and reputable sources. The internet is an excellent resource since there are plenty of free resources like Success Magazine, Business Insider as well as Forbes Magazine who each have an inventory of startups to research. In addition, Linkedin, the professional social media platform, will provide you a list of startups to look into. Through gaining an understanding of the companies that are currently in the process of starting up it will help you know more about what it is like to be a part of a business such as this.

You will get a better understanding of the roles the companies are trying to fill by doing some research online. You'll be able to get an understanding of the abilities as well as the responsibilities and expectations they require from the candidates they select. This can help you start to consider how the abilities you already possess could be adapted to an opening at a start-up. Apply to these job advertisements, but times, start-ups only post a small amount in terms of positions they're looking to fill. The simple act of looking for work is not going to get you a major breakthrough into the start-up world.

The majority of people who work for an start-up have had their names circulated through the hands of someone they know. It could be a friend of an old colleague, or a distant family member whoever it is that you know and obtaining an introduction is the most effective method to gain entry into the startup world. Contrary to traditional companies which rely on referrals to assist you on paper and you'll be selected based on your work experience and previous work experience, in an entrepreneur-driven company your skills and experience will not be noticed if you do not have an existing foot into the company's door.

The process of launching a startup is easier if you reside in one of the most well-known tech startup cities such as New York City, San Francisco, Seattle, Austin and Denver. These cities that are highly desirable for startups offer those who are looking to make it in the industry many opportunities to get their name known. But, they're not the only cities where startups are growing or are thriving. There's a possibility that regardless of where you live, there's an established startup community that you can start to make connections within. There's also a high chance of knowing someone else who has a connection with someone else working in the startup world.

Being a part of this intimate community begins with making contact with who you already have in common. Networking is often viewed as a benefit and a negative for those looking to get a job at an emerging company. It is a benefit because it can take you out of your comfortable area, you'll encounter new and exciting people, and can frequently lead to unending opportunities that you thought of not getting. The disadvantage to networking is it usually isn't for all. It is necessary to work on your social skills, and it takes time to establish those relationships with appropriate people. If you're bold determined, persistent, and ready to be out there consistently and make the most of every opportunity, it will be easy.

Building your network

Networking requires you to become comfortable with discomfort. It's going to require you to go out there , and participating in talks, seminars, meetups and many more. You will also need to conduct research, making connections that are not often made and then taking actions. Networking is the initial step, and usually the most crucial and rewarding action to take as you begin looking for work in the startup world.

There are many networking events that are held all over the world. There are plenty of opportunities to find out more about the industry of start-ups or to learn the skills needed to enter into a startup through different workshops, events and seminars. You should take the time to go to as many of these kinds of events as you can. Certain of these events might not appeal to you in the slightest. If you're not a tech-savvy person, the coding workshop or an introduction to data analysis is an uninteresting wasted time. Even if you're not interested in learning how to code or data analysis it is among the most effective ways to get an introduction to the fundamental concept of what create a successful tech start-up. This will also allow you to get acquainted with people who might already have an established presence in the technology start-up world.

If you are active and participating in events, even if they may not excite you to the fullest You will be able to make new acquaintances and connections. In addition to going to these events, might want to check if they offer volunteers. Through volunteering, you might be able to connect with a greater quantity of people. You don't know where one interaction could lead to. Keep an open mind and be keen to learn what you have to know to get into the business.

Another method to meet those that are looking to join the start-up business is to reach out to people you have in common. It is easy to reconnect with your former acquaintances via social media. Sending a simple message to keep in touch with them may make it easier to connect with people who work in the startup business. Also, don't be afraid to contact people you know who are in the business. LinkedIn is a fantastic platform to meet with startup founders or investors as well as others who work in the field. Sending a short message to ask for advice or getting feedback from is an excellent way to begin conversations and could result in the possibility of a job offer.

Some tips to remember when you're building your list of contacts.

Be sure to keep in touch. One of the most damaging ways to lose contact is to let your connection dwindle out. If someone invites you on an evening coffee or provides you with all the info you require to start a new business, you should make sure you make contact with them frequently. Even if nothing happens from the initial connection the regular chance that a person you know may lead you to connect with someone else and that person could offer you a chance.

Always maintain a positive outlook. It isn't a good idea to enter every conversation with the expectation that you will get something useful from this relationship however, you need to remember that anything could happen. If you dismiss someone because you don't think they could offer something, you're missing the purpose of networking. You should remain optimistic but not be entangled by the results.

Consider what you could help them. One of the most effective methods of establishing a strong relationship, especially with the founder is to let them know the things you can offer them. Perhaps you have ideas for marketing, content you've written or potential in a market that they haven't yet targeted yet. If you begin conversation by providing value to your company and not expecting anything in return, it will not go unnoticed. Be aware that every interaction that you make is one-way. Even if it's simply chatting and racking the brains of someone working within the business, you should be thinking about ways to help them also.

The first step is to get your foot in the starting-up door.

In addition to building networks, another method to make yourself known to an organization you're attracted to is following them on each platform they're present on. You can share their content, give them a shout-out or leave a comment, and show that you're curious about what they're doing. Every startup will have a presence on social media typically across multiple platforms By showing an that you are interested in them on these platforms, you're already making your brand be noticed.

If you first show your interest by expressing your interest, you could be more at ease to send them a message. It is possible to mention that you've been sharing your information, promoted the product, and that you have several people who are attracted by what they do and your desire to work more things with them. This is a straightforward approach which demonstrates to the new company the various aspects of what you're about. It suggests that you are engaged in what the business is up to. It also shows that are enthusiastic and ready to take charge. In addition, it indicates that you're eager to create more value and achieve results.

To be able to get your foot in the right direction, you have to be prepared to complete the work. It can be a lengthy process, but it usually has the highest reward. Also, you should think about making a difference to the businesses that you're interested in before making a request for a job or contacting them.

Chapter 9: How to Create A Good

Cash Flow for Your business

We all know that businesses can't survive in the absence of a constant cash flow. There will be occasions that cash flow is likely to be scarce. There are times where the company will be growing and you'll get plenty of cash flow through the process. To ensure that your finances remain steady, you must be able manage your business effectively.

How Do You Plan to Control Your Cash Flow?

To do this make note of the followingpoints:

You must be aware of the funds that's coming into your business from various businesses and the costs that you will have to incur. Check if the amount is flowing out and in is correct and if you are overspending, look for ways to cut down on the cash flow of your business.

Prepare a cash flow forecast. If you're unfamiliar about this, it's an extensive report on possible costs and the amount of money the company could have within a specified amount of time. Be aware that this report should be carried out regularly to aid in the management of your finances. You should be able to include in your report every transaction you've completed, regardless of regardless of whether the transaction involves money going out or money coming in. Account records from banks may be required in this case.

Be realistic about an effort to manage your money. You can't put the ideal and worst scenarios to your financial situation. It is important to ensure that you're sticking to the scenario you consider to be the most likely. The reason to make this decision is that this way, you'll be able to anticipate what will happen over the coming months or even weeks. Some people have a difficult time making predictions, particularly if the company is new, and the products offered for sale to customers are not old also. The best way to make it easier to predict the future is to invest in software. You might think it won't be helpful, but it can. You just need to input all the information you have and the program will take over making predictions of your cash flow.

Consider that one method by that you can boost cash flow is to make sure you look after clients that pay in time or even earlier. They're helping your business and so the best thing to do is ensure that they receive perks too. Offer discounts that don't affect the profit of your company but will increase your cash flow dramatically.

It could be an excellent idea to make sure the flow of cash is able to be steady, but there are times that this isn't the case. To boost your flow of money, you need to figure out the factors that are causing you to fall. Make these improvements as your money flow will definitely improve over the next couple of months or more.

Cash No Money No Cash No Way!

The advantages of bartering your company

Sales increase

Businesses make use of barter systems to buy different products or services they require. They make payments using the products or services they provide. If you're a part of a barter exchange network your business gets presented to more companies. These businesses could be potential customers. Along with your current customers, they can assist your business expand and generate more sales.

Cash is saved

This is among the main goals of bartering in the business. Bartering is a system of exchange, when you need raw materials, products or services, you don't have to make payments in cash. You can trade your own goods to meet the requirements. This way, you can conserve cash and capital to invest in other areas of your business.

Bartering is also a factor in decreasing operating costs, cash flow and overhead expenses. Services like housekeeping, travel accounting, and advertising come in the category of overhead expenses. There are a lot of dollars that could be saved by acquiring these services via barter.

Improve management of inventory

If your business is in the midst of having excess stocks and raw materials sitting idle and won't be useful in the near future You can trade the items for more valuable and essential items or services. Particularly during times of economic downturn getting rid of the unneeded and surplus inventory to gain other resources that are more essential can be beneficial.

Purchase Advertising and Media

The key to any business's success is its publicity and promotion through any kind of media. In many cases one thing which can stop a business from enjoying the fruits of its labor is the proper execution for an advertisement campaign. You can make use of barter to incorporate different types of media, such as print, TV,

Online Social Media etc. as part of your business plan.

Another thing to consider is bartering

Avoid banksrupt partners

You should barter with businesses that are performing well. Be cautious about entering into an agreement to barter with a company that is spiraling to bankruptcy, since it could be that you don't get your fair share in the event that everything goes downhill for the bartering party.

Tax issues

Bartering is not an opportunity to get around tax liability. Bartering earnings are subject to taxation during the year during which the products and services are purchased. In accordance with the law that govern it, the earnings must be declared.

It should be connected to the business

The products or services purchased via barter need to be appropriate and contribute the value of your company. For instance, you might not necessarily get the same amount from a homekeeping service that you can get through barter as through an advertisement service. If your goods or services aren't popular, you might want to join an exchange group for barter.

Barter Exchange Groups

There are many barter exchange organizations today, where you can choose a suitable barter partner to sell your services and goods to purchase other services. A majority of barter exchanges are profit-driven. Therefore, you need to choose the one that has affordable membership fees and benefits.

While you may not always be able to trade in barter for items you need, in times of economic hardship and recession, it could definitely help you save money.

How can you expand your business online using LinkedIn

LinkedIn could play an crucial role in the promotion campaign for your company. In recent times, many companies are using LinkedIn as a cost-free marketing tool to advertise their products. In contrast to Facebook marketing on LinkedIn is an approach that is more professional by analyzing your existing and potential contacts and including them in your marketing campaigns.

It is equally important to connect with your LinkedIn profile through your social media interactions and activities, while using LinkedIn as a way to keep contacts up to date with your latest products and services. Here are some crucial aspects to think about when deciding on your marketing plan for LinkedIn.

All employees of your company to create an LinkedIn profile and connect with one another. The networking process can lead to boost exposure for the organization. If someone is reluctant to make an account, help them realize that it's an essential requirement for professional today nearly every big corporate shot has an account on LinkedIn.

Make sure you link your company's websites and blogs to the details of your LinkedIn profile. Visitors to your site can look over the contents of your LinkedIn profile and see your profile and see any suggestions that you have received. It helps them build a stronger connection to your company. However, it is recommended to have profiles of the top management on your company's website. In addition each employee in your business can be able to link back to your website. If someone visits your profile and would like to know what you can offer, they are able to go to your company's website directly from there. To ensure security from a search engine viewpoint it is best to link to your LinkedIn profile on your site as a no-follow hyperlink.

Another approach you could think about is creating your own company profile on LinkedIn. Include your company's name and all relevant information to make your page more efficient. Continue posting regularly informing your followers about the latest products or services, and also publishing informative and valuable content to your website.

Incorporate popular phrases or keywords that are relevant to your business on your personal profile or website page for your company. If you're planning to run an online advertising campaign, ensure that you use the same keywords used on your business page on your advertisements too. This will give a consistent look to your business , and helps make your business appear more professional.

Create a forum for your company , if it falls in the services category. If your business offers services to a specific industry or has a well-known name on the web this could be a great place for your customers or contacts to talk about various developments in the field. Engage members by launching discussions and posting announcements about new offerings , or other developments or changes that are related to your company.

Finally be sure to build strong connections with your business partners and all media connections. On LinkedIn you can choose who you would like to connect with and whom you should make your business's goals. You should try to establish connections with businesses who could benefit from your services or products. Consider establishing connections with journalists and bloggers who are covering your sector.

While marketing through LinkedIn requires a longer approach and a professional approach, the ability to create solid relationships is well worth the effort. Connecting with and focusing on the people you connect with is important in the social media world but it is also able to produce incredible results in the long run.

The Simple Wealth Generation Plan

When it comes to the notion of running a business, many people don't think about the magnitude of the financial investment or the commitment to time required to stand a good chance of success. It is effortless to be caught in the excitement of success "potential" when the hope that you'll be successful is a must and should be tempered by a solid plan and resources.

We're aware that you'll need to have a significant amount of cash to even think about running an establishment like a McDonald's. A friend of mine was seeking to start a cell phone company and after looking into her options , we found that at the lower end of the spectrum, you will require $25,000 upfront and an additional

$5,000 per month until profits cover expenses.

The other alternative was T-Mobile with a liquid capital in the amount of 1.5 million dollars, and the ambition to open 10 stores with such a strong brand you could imagine achieving success in three to five years. But how many entrepreneurs do you know have this amount of money tucked away?

The plan below after several revisions was provided and ratified. I'm sharing what I know offer, and giving you the framework to show that this could be used for virtually any big business idea you have in mind.

Buy or build an online site in line with the type of company you are looking to launch

Create a strong marketing strategy to promote your business online

Put money into expanding your company's success i.e. leads, sales and top quality products and services

Develop at minimum 1-10 additional websites with a similar niche that have the same target market

Cross-promote your income-generating network of websites

Expand your business by increasing the marketing

Make sure that the process you are using is automated and self-generating.

You can form an entire group (outsource) with a pay package which includes bonuses based on team members bringing in more profit.

Make an online website for your business One of the primary reasons for establishing a profitable modern-day Start-up is easy and powerful. If you've got an idea for a business why not get it started by putting it online?

Using the knowledge and experience gained from building site after site for clients, as well as creating companies, products, and services for MyUSAMediaGroup.com's multidimensional media marketing campaigns. We use a straightforward strategy for developing each site specific to the specific niche:

We always place F.I.R.S.T first!

Be sure to focus on the primary goal of the website is in sales, lead generation or informational

Put money into a plan of business for your site that is based on this model

Discover the top companies on the internet

Choose components you enjoy from successful companies that match the purpose of your site. Then, incorporate the elements you like into your site and your business over time.

Keep investing in items which can increase or sustain your earnings while increasing your market share, essentially making more people aware about your company's products and services.

Another option we would recommend and use is to purchase websites online depending on the kind of company you want to establish. If you make use of the same data you've been provided to purchase a site, you can acquire the hard work and efforts of another taking a couple of steps further down the process. Based on the amount of development and effort has been put into the developed project, you could purchase an existing business that is profitable and expand it from its current location.

Once you have a great website, you need to make or follow a well-constructed marketing strategy and invest as the money you can in expanding your company i.e. leads, increasing sales and producing more top quality items or products.

When it comes to running an online business, you can concentrate your marketing efforts on gaining specific traffic. The more potential customers who can benefit from the product you offer who visit your website the better, regardless of the business model you choose to run.

If your site is performing better and has a solid foundation, you can increase your investment in other niche-related websites in the same market.

Consider the life cycle of your client and offer additional value and develop your websites to serve a different area of the market you have been successful in.

One good example of this is our business model . We have a media firm myusamediagroup.com which creates marketing campaigns. We also have myusalocal.com which provides an added value to the community with an increasing number of targeted customers that businesses want to reach out to. If you search, we have numerous websites that offer content across the internet that allow us to reach very specific individuals who are looking for the information and products or services associated with the websites.

We also own publishing as well as other product creation properties. These virtual businesses make it simple to work at a larger capacity, while also increasing the quality of our products for our users.

Now that you've the synergy of several companies or websites that feed into each other whenever feasible, you will be able to increase your results by promoting your income-generating network.

Expand your business by increasing your marketing efforts once you're certain that your Process is fully automated.

Think of your company as an task until it is able to run without you there. It is possible to start as soon as you're financially capable to hire a team of employees to manage your business.

Being a trainer and coach I not only build teams (outsource) capable of handling the day-to-day tasks to pay my clients, I also provide bonuses that are based on the team's performance, which increases the profits.

Even if all you write down is the steps you follow to run your business and hire an occasional VA to take care of certain aspects of your business, you're superior to the majority of entrepreneurs.

Chapter 10: The Mistakes to Avoid in

Client Relationships

The biggest error coaches make when it comes to their work has to do getting too familiar with their clients.

Family ties breed disdain.

Friends don't pay each other to coach them. Friends support each other for no cost. If you don't benefit from friendship. You lose it.

The only people you are able to exert less control over than your friends are your family members.

Your customers aren't able to call you like your family or friends could. You should limit access. Also, there must be something special in what you do.

When they believe they've got everything they need from you, and the second they believe they have all the answers you know, they're gone. They'll lose interest in you in such a way that your mind will spin.

This is the reason you have to be extremely cautious of what you are letting your clients know, and what they see, and what you won't allow them to know about. If you do meet regularly with them in person it is important to be extremely cautious about the amount of time spent with them, where they get to see more more of your real self and less and less the carefully constructed image we have discussed in the earlier part of this book.

Then, you should not be obligated at any cost. You don't want people to feel as if they are bound to you. You don't want to feel any commitments to your customers.

If you have to meet the clients you serve at a location such as a restaurant, make sure you pay the bill. This is an important practice because it's symbolic. It reveals a variety of things about the person you are.

It is not a good idea to profit unfairly of a customer. It's okay for them to perform a task for you every once in time, but you shouldn't have them work for you at no cost for a week in consecutive weeks.

Your customers should desire to be just like you. It could be a puzzle to you why one would desire to emulate you, particularly when they earn more that you. They want to emulate you due to the behaviors they observe as well as the confidence, discipline and control behavior.

They don't want to be just like them and they won't choose them as a coach if you're crying and weak and complain and whine as well. Your relationships have been broken up too. And everyone in your team is a fool. And your customers are as well. There is no one who wants to be the same as you. They will also think they can't offer any advice that is helpful that could mean the end of life to your company.

You shouldn't be discussing such things with your clients who you coach. You shouldn't be able to talk about or complain to the clients of yours in ways which hinder their desire to be similar to you.

Another mistake coaches on the internet make is believing that their continued participation in your coaching programs as well as patronage of your business , and the interest of your clients are a sign of gratitude for the past contributions you've contributed as coach. It's not the case.

Everyone hopes this is the case but it isn't the case. Your memories for your clients who you coach online are extremely small. They may also be inclined to alter the past and their memories in their minds , which can diminish the significance of your contribution to their achievements.

If you'd like to keep your clients on your coaching program for a long period of time Here's what you can do Clients will continue to participation in your coaching programs in a way that is more influenced by their emotions instead of the facts. The the reality could be filled with great achievements and positive results for them.

Coaching business online is a feeling-based business. It's about how your clients think about you, how they perceive themselves as well as what they think about the experiences they have while participating within your program of coaching. It's not about getting tangible results.

Customers will depart depending on their impressions, even if they are actually achieving amazing results. If you earn one million dollars, and they aren't enjoying themselves with you the person will quit you.

You should carefully consider how you can influence, control and control the emotions of your clients who you coach. Your business is all about the way they feel, not the outcomes.

You must be able to show results, but the difference between average outcomes and exceptional results won't lead to better retention. Retention isn't based on outcomes. The retention comes from the way your customers feel about your business.

Another mistake is providing too much information. Some coaches believe that they can keep clients longer by delivering more information. They also add webinars. They have five skype calls instead 3 skype call.

The rest of the things don't really matter because there's enough. It is possible that you have too little content However, eventually the accumulation of additional content won't be enough help you solve retention issues. Additionally there will be people who begin to leave when you offer excessive content.

They may feel as if they aren't able to go through the whole thing. It means they'll are feeling stupid, and nobody likes to feel foolish.

If people experience negative emotions They try to move as far as they can from what is causing the negative emotions. They do not attempt to change their actions, they just leave. If you're causing negative emotions, they will be fleeing from them.

Chapter 11: Making Your Startup

Look Like It's On The Map

The location of your business is a crucial factor that will be a major factor in the success of your business! It's not as simple as simply picking an empty office or storefront and not paying much attention. As with all aspects of starting your own business choosing a place to locate your venture will require some time and effort.

General Questions

When you're deciding on an area, you'll have think beyond dimensions or attractive looks. You should consider the relevance of the location to the target market as well as its proximity to suppliers, the ease of access, and how it is with respect to its other competitors. It is important not to be too close or too far from your competitors. You'll need to consider the accessibility of pedestrians and parking, and the potential of the possibility of special event traffic. Startups that create software for corporate clients will likely be fine by locating a small office located in a quiet part of a park for corporate clients however, this won't work for a clothing store that depends on walk-ins pedestrian traffic, and even the ability to make impulse sales to survive. For the latter, they'll require an expansive area that is well-lit and close to other shops and accessible on the foot or via a vehicle.

A great place can be the difference between success and failure for your business. It's not practical nor efficient to just be apprehensive and hope that you can find a suitable inexpensive location, particularly when you are preparing to launch your business. In this scenario it is highly recommended that you seek out and benefit from working with a commercial real estate agent. The less urgent schedules can be accommodated through search on your local Craigslist or other on social media "for for sale" forums, and via the local branch of a small-business group.

Many start-ups rent space in the beginning because they anticipate that their business will rapidly grow until they require something larger. You may happen to stumble upon the ideal location on your own, however, before you leap at the chance, be aware of the following factors.

Accessibility

Which is your audience is located relative to your area? Since a bar that serves sports would likely draw young adults and college students and young adults, it is unlikely to do well if it were to open in an area that is primarily populated with elderly people. Similar to that an elderly housing complex will probably not attract a lot of people living in the midst of fraternity row close to the campus of a university. A location that is relevant to your target market is crucial, particularly since it's now easy to find the closest to any business of any type.

Financial Factors

Any business that requires an establishment with a physical storefront must review its financial position to ensure it is able to afford the space needed to accommodate exhibit, showcase, and present the products it sells to prospective customers. However an operation that is based on services might require little or any space and is referred to as a remote site.

Certain kinds of businesses could benefit from mobile websites for example, food trucks, mall kiosks or food trucks. Keep in mind that you're not bound to your initial place forever. You will be able to move to bigger premises when your company expands. The most important thing is to select a location that is in line with the federal and state standards for your particular industry We'll discuss the details on a couple of pages, so you don't need to worry about them immediately.

Does it support your brand?

A crucial aspect to think about when selecting a area is how well it conveys your brand. There are a variety of ways you can show your brand's image through the specifics of your location and the architecture. For instance, certain Disney stores feature sparkling floors, specifically designed to reflect the innocent excitement that the Disney brand inspires in its customers of all different ages. A lot of fast food establishments employ an exclusive interior color scheme that transmits an implicit message to their customers to eat food and then get moving by aligning their physical location to the concept that they are "fast" meals. The structures that house the sites to host Medieval Times, a business that reenacts medieval festivals and tournaments designed to resemble castles, and thus entice customers to fully immerse themselves in the world of during Medieval Times. Middle Ages.

How Close is the Competition

How close is your potential area to your competitors? In my early teen years I worked in the fast food chain for a few summers. A few days ago, our grill was damaged and we were unable offer burgers, regardless of the fact that they were our most popular selling factor. In the afternoon, a group of people came in and I shared the negatives of our grill. I also explained the menu options we had available. They were debating what to do, when one of their friends told them, "Hey, there's a pizza and cheese steak restaurant close to on the same street." I'm certain you'll be able to determine the place they went to for lunch!

Imagine the day when you're not able give your customers what you've promised them. For the area you're thinking of where do they have to travel to receive what they're looking for? If your competition is close enough, you'll be at risk of losing to them.

But, it's crucial to consider it from the other perspective. What would you do if you were owner of the cheesesteak restaurant? You'd just acquired two new customers because the competition could not give them the service they required. If you offer a unique experience that is superior to your competition, you might be able to win the customer's loyalty for life!

If your competition is close It can be for your benefit, so provided you're well-prepared. This can be a great way to motivate you to remain at the top of your game and ensure that your operations are running regularly.

Are there nearby companies that could help increase sales for your business? This is a great approach. If, for instance, you're an auto parts store that is situated across next to a mechanic shop it's highly likely that the mechanic that owns this repair business will eventually become your client since he'll always require auto parts.

How close are You to Suppliers?

You should also think about your current location in terms of the distance you're located with your supplier. In the above example the mechanic is close to a possible supplier and the auto parts shop is close by. I live just next to a wholesaler of produce that supplies fresh, local-grown fruits and vegetables to local restaurants as well as supermarkets within a 10-mile distance. This means that my neighborhood supermarket is always full of the latest produce and vegetables!

The advantages of working with local suppliers is that it creates bonds with a particular community. It also eases the process of locating what you require within a short time, which allows you to service your customers faster. I've seen restaurant owners rush to a nearby store in rare instances when they're running out in products. Being close to suppliers can mean the difference between an enthusiastic customer and one who waits for the item to arrivedue to the sheer need.

If the products you require aren't readily accessible, you can opt to have them delivered the delivery service that is overnight. In this instance the proximity of major roads will be an important factor. While you search for your new location, you should ask yourself what items you'll need frequently. You can then choose the ideal location based on how fast suppliers are able to reach you. If you are primarily dependent on deliveries that take a long time the most important thing is how easy it is for drivers to get to your home, specifically the loading area. You'll be able to see how Walmart stores are located nearer to the closest major highway. This is done to maximize their profits since the majority of what they sell is transported via semi trailers.

It is also crucial to think about the accessibility to your business. How many times have you attempted to go to a place of business and found that parking was difficult to locate? Then you probably quit and went to a different establishment with more parking options.

Businesses that are hard to find drive me nuts. Once I was asked to an interview. I put an address in my map and drove for 40 minutes to the place. When I finally arrived, I was unsure of which way to go, as there were no signs in the building to signal the entrance. Nor was there an address label or something to show what the business's name was. company. I ended up driving away, frustrated.

Visibility

What is visibility? A number of times, I've walked past an establishment in the area which caught my eye when I was on my way to another place. I'd think, "That place looks interesting and I'm definitely going to go there very soon!" What caught my interest was not just the location, but also the possibility of seeing the name of the business clearly.

If you choose to put your company on a bustling main street, it could let you enjoy the benefits of the traffic. If you opt to set up your business on a minor street corner, it is unlikely that you'll get as much traffic drop-in.

If you're located in a bigger city, you should take into consideration potential customers who do not own a car. Are you easily accessible via public transport? Is it safe for someone to reach your establishment on a bicycle? By foot?

The street you're situated on can have a major impact on. If, for instance, the majority of the traffic along that street is left-hand and your business is not on the right, it may not be able to benefit from locating on the right-hand side of the street. If you have the coffee shop that has a drive-through it is a good idea to benefit from locating your business on the side of the road with the most morning traffic!

The Angle of Safety Angle

Security is a crucial aspect to consider when choosing your next place of business, both for the employees you employ and your customers. Do not be afraid to research the statistics of crime of your prospective location and consider yourself in the position of your customers. Would you like to visit an establishment in a location which is a danger in the evening? If you're in a highly-crime area it's likely that you'll lose the evening sales, and will have a difficult finding employees for in the night shift. What about an area that is difficult at any time throughout the day? Would your customers be willing to risk their lives in order to get access to your products or services?

The Stability Of The Property

If you've found a place which is ideal for your venture take care to inquire about the past of the place and current condition. Image is crucial for any company. If you are operating from an area that's falling in disrepair, that you will not be able to gain the trust of your customers. They could be worried about their safety and would be hesitant to set their feet in your building. At the minimum they'd find it difficult to judge the quality of what you're providing them. Older buildings usually require more money for maintenance and you'll need to consider this. Older properties may not likely to be able to handle the current electrical loads of equipment , and might not be equipped with the latest technology, like Wi-Fi.

Asking about the background of the area can save both time and cash. You should approach the ownership and renting process with a wide-open mind. If you discover that a space is available due to previous businesses that did not succeed there then you should take the time to find out why exactly that they were unsuccessful. There may be another reason for the failures which isn't related to the businesses that failed.

In my home town there was a building along the highway that was an Ice cream shop for a long time. When the ice cream store left, a swift series of companies opened and shut down within 5 years. Why? There was a rumor that circulated around city that this building had been infested by termites. If real or false, the story pretty much sounded the death knell of any business that dared to open a shop in the area.

It's important to learn about the history of the building before signing the"dotted line. This is the time when an agent for real estate can prove to be invaluable. A person who is knowledgeable about the area is knowledgeable details about the history of the property as well as the past owner and tenant.

Legalities to Take into Consideration

Be aware of the legal aspects of deciding on your location. Before you choose a space be sure to check if the area is licensed as commercial usage. It is easy to find this information by calling local office of the government. Some homes are residential, which means they can be used to only residential use. It is possible to seek out a property located in an area that is zoned to commercial uses. Certain zones are also zoned for mixed-use properties, so it's not always possible to determine a property's condition just by watching its neighbors.

Another situation where an agent for real estate can help: any licensed agent ought to be able to verify the zoned status of a property. If you're searching for properties on your own However, you'll be required to contact the local authorities to verify that you're permitted to conduct business from that particular area.

It is also important to find out the permits or licenses you must obtain before opening your doors to businesses. This may require a meeting with local officials, in addition to an inquiry from your industry. For instance the restaurant will most likely require a letter of approval by a local health official. Additionally, it would require at the very least one of its employees to be certified as safe for food prior to launching operations. Certain businesses, like salons, require specific permits and require certificates of each employee. There is a chance that you'll need the approval of an inspector from the local fire department before you are able to let your business open for public viewing.

As I've previously mentioned you'll need to make sure you have access to delivery at your residence. If you're located in a commercial structure that is situated near in a residential zone, most likely, those living in the area will want to know that you aren't disrupting their streets or making loud deliveries during the night.

A major convenience store just opened up for business just down the street my home. While the property is zoned for commercial use, it's right next to the residential street. Residents who lived on the street were worried about the disruption caused by large trucks that bring in deliveries as well as the security of their children playing in the vicinity of these vehicles, as well as the inconvenience of big semis that were blocking the street. After meeting with residents, the business was able to reach an agreement that was in line with all the requirements of the town. They agreed to accept only deliveries at night which successfully addressed their demands.

Since different permits/licenses/certifications are required for different industries, states, and municipalities, I cannot outline their details here. You must conduct your own research and research to discover the specifics of what you must complete before you are able to officially start business.

Assistance with Pesky Details

After you've located the ideal place to start your business however, there are some things to consider prior to signing a lease contract or buy agreement. Be aware of the long-term cost implications of property taxes and utilities, insurance maintenance, future expansion and even issues of aesthetics like the color scheme of your furniture, paint and other elements of décor. It is important to make sure that your budget is adequate for any remodel that might be needed prior to the grand opening.

Yes, location hunting may be a daunting undertaking however, don't give up hope. It's good to know that your lawyer will usually assist you during this procedure. A lawyer is necessary to scrutinize contracts prior to you sign them. He will assist you in your negotiations to negotiate the most favorable leasing terms and assist you in dealing the landlord. The majority of landlords are great for working with however occasionally you'll come across one who's happy to share with your lawyer!

A commercial realtor could be an excellent resource when searching for a suitable location for your company. Commercial real estate agents is a specialist of the local area and the people who live there. Commercial realtors are in a position to assist you to determine the best place based on your needs for your property as well as the client base you'll serve.

Do not be reluctant to seek the help of these professionals. They are worth the price of gold. They can help you avoid numerous problems, and they can also keep you from making choices that you'll regret later on. Take their recommendations. Consider a second opinion if you're required however, keep in mind that you're paying for their experience and wisdom. Get the most out of these relationships and you'll be glad you did.

Chapter 12: Facebook Tips to

Increase Traffic to Increase Your

Fanbase

If you were to ask different people what social media site they consider to be one of the top, you'll likely get the answer "Facebook" many times. There are millions of users using it each and every day. In reality it has seen more than one billion account accounts made since the start of Facebook. Furthermore, there are numerous people who make Facebook accounts each day.

Some were created by people who want to make the opportunity to make a fresh start, while some want to create accounts for marketing to customers. Whatever the motivation for establishing an account, there are plenty of users who use Facebook to check out things that might spark their curiosity.

This is likely the reason that the majority of people today setting up Facebook accounts for their own companies. They know they'll be able reach many more people via this channel. If you consider it even if you have a webpage, it doesn't mean that everyone will be interested in your site or be interested in the content you provide.

If you'd like to join Facebook to increase more followers or to gain more followers, what are you able to do?

Facebook Graph Search is very beneficial to local businesses, and , along the Facebook's Edge Rank can get you an effective start with advertising your company.

Things You Can Do to Increase Your Followers on Facebook:

Before you get involved in the various enhancements, think about your intended audience first. What are the types of people you'd like to see become interested in your website, business product, or product.

Include the physical address of your business when you create your page. Also, make sure you choose the appropriate category for your company.

If you are planning to start an event, you could begin by giving prizes would be interesting to people. The requirements they must to do to participate can be linked to help you gain followers. For instance, they must be asked to share your website and while doing so make sure that some of their friends follow your page too. This will increase the number of fans, and eventually make your page go viral.

Be sure to include an like box on your site and include the exact address you have for your business appear on the page, and vice versa to.

As with other social networking websites, you'll need to develop tags to make your company easy to find. It is always possible to gain followers by sharing and tagging things that are related to the services you offer and selling for the public at large. You shouldn't tag something simply because they're present on your website. You'll only be able to get people offended by this method.

Imagine an "Foursquare" kind of marketing strategy, which allows your patrons to check in on Facebook whenever they're at your place of business and provide incentives such as discounts, discounts, etc.

Because you're only starting out It's not a bad idea to run Facebook promoted search results. If you are able to do this, they'll also suggest you to those they believe would be interested in the services you offer. This will depend on what they declare their interests to be and who your ideal customer is.

Conclusion

If you're unsure whether you could begin your own business in the comfort of your home or at work there is no reason to be the only one. There are plenty of people who haven't decided to regain the reins of their finances because they believe they're not "experts" or knowledgeable enough about their field to start a business that is their own.

Let go of this mentality by accepting that, yes you're not an expert but you can turn into one! With the vastness that is the Internet, you can access many resources available to help you learn more about the company you're planning to start. It's up to you to start the process.

I'm hoping that this book was helpful and will provide you with the necessary tools to reach your goals of financial freedom while you get rid of the chains of the typical 9-5 job!

Next step to select the business model you liked studying about. What kind of business attracted your attention the most? If there are multiple types, note them down and do some research to learn more. Find your own way to think! There's no reason to believe that you shouldn't be able to combine ideas well! You're the only one setting limits for yourself.